BOOK BUDDIES™

A Program of The Molina Foundation

A Book about a Boy Living with AIDS

Carmine's Story

*Text and photographs
by Arlene Schulman*

LERNER PUBLICATIONS COMPANY / MINNEAPOLIS

The author gives special thanks to Lori Wiener of the National Cancer Institute.

Illustrations by John Erste

LIBRARY OF CONGRESS CATALOGING-IN-PUBLICATION DATA

Schulman, Arlene.
   Carmine's story : a book about a boy living with AIDS / text and photographs by Arlene Schulman.
   p. cm.
   Includes bibliographical references (p. 38)
   Summary: A ten-year-old AIDS patient describes the disease, how he got it, and how it is affecting his daily life.
   ISBN 0-8225-2582-8 (alk. paper)
   1. Buete, Carmine, 1986–1996—Health. 2. AIDS (Disease) in children—Patients—New York (State)—Queens (New York)—Biography—Juvenile literature. [1. AIDS (Disease)—Patients.] I. Title.
RJ387.A25B847 1997
362.1'98929792'0092
[b]—DC20   96-41716

Manufactured in the United States of America
1 2 3 4 5 6 – JR – 02 01 00 99 98 97

CONTENTS

"For nearly every American with eyes and ears open, the face of AIDS is no longer the face of a stranger."

—*President Bill Clinton*

MY NAME IS CARMINE. I'm ten years old, and I have AIDS.

My mother had AIDS, too. Her name was Florence. She died when I was a year and three months old. I don't really remember her. But sometimes when the wind blows the front door open, I say that it's my mother.

I don't know who my father is. My mother never told anyone, not even her mother. We think he might have been from Puerto Rico, but we're not sure. Wherever he is, he doesn't know me.

My grandmother, Kay, told me that my mother was her favorite. She was fun and she liked to talk and she could make friends with anybody. Then she met a man—maybe it was my father—who was using drugs. She started to use drugs, too. I don't know why. I wish I could ask her.

My mother used a drug called heroin before I was born. She injected it into her body with needles. She and her boyfriend shared their needles with other people, and one of them must have had AIDS. That's how I think my mother got the disease.

When my mother found out she was going to have a baby, she stopped using drugs right away. She wanted to be a good mom. But it was too late. The AIDS virus had already passed from her to me.

I live with my grandmother in Ozone Park, Queens. It's not far from New York City. I call my grandmother Mom. It's just the two of us. We live in a house that New York City provides for people with AIDS. My house has a living room, a bedroom for me and one for my grandmother, a kitchen, and a bathroom. It also has a small porch and a yard where we put our clothes out to dry when the weather is nice.

My room is my favorite place. I have lots of toys and games. My favorite game is Monopoly. I also play all kinds of video games and watch movies on tape. I like karate and all the karate movies. I've been to Disneyland, and I like going to the circus. My favorite toy is my E.T. doll. It makes me feel better when I'm sick. E.T. takes the sickness away.

I get tired easily. When that happens, I just lie in my bed and rest or I take a nap on the couch. Sometimes the medicine I take makes me moody. Then I get kind of quiet and I don't want to talk to anyone. I don't like it when that happens.

SOMETIMES I FEEL BAD for my grandmother. One of her sons, my uncle Chuck, also has AIDS. He got it from using drugs. He says that he's going to fight it, though. I like to play cards with Chuck. He came to live with my grandmother because she knows how to care for people with AIDS.

Another member of the family, Ricky, also died of AIDS. He was a stockbroker and he was gay. That means he was interested in dating men. He got AIDS from another man.

My grandmother is a very strong person. She's 67 years old. She says that taking care of us is no big deal. But when she thinks no one sees her, she goes underneath the covers to cry.

AIDS is not something that happens only to gay men and people who have used drugs. It can affect anyone.

Most kids get AIDS from their mothers. We were infected before we were born because our mothers had the AIDS virus in their bodies. A few kids have gotten AIDS from blood transfusions, but that's pretty rare, because blood supplies in the United States are tested thoroughly to make sure the blood is safe.

Kids from all over the world have AIDS, from Africa to India, Ireland, the Caribbean, China, Russia, the United States, and other countries. If these kids got the virus from their mothers, then maybe they are being raised by their grandmothers, like I am.

AIDS is caused by the human immunodeficiency virus, or HIV. HIV kills cells in your blood called T cells. T cells help fight illnesses and diseases. A healthy person has more than 800 T cells per cubic millimeter of blood. I have none. I haven't had any for the last five years, so I need to be very careful about germs. If I were to catch a cold, my body would not be able to stop the infection. The cold could turn into something worse, like pneumonia. And that could kill me.

People can't catch AIDS by kissing me or hugging me or borrowing my pencil. The AIDS virus can only live inside a person's body. You can get the disease by having sex with an infected person, like my uncle did, or by sharing needles to use drugs, like my mother did. A mother can pass the virus to her child before birth or at the time of birth, which is how I got it.

There's a blood test that tells you if you have the virus. If you do, you are "HIV positive." When you start to develop symptoms like pneumonia or other illnesses, then you have AIDS. It usually takes about ten years before someone with the virus develops AIDS. But it's different for every person. For kids, it usually takes about two years.

I've had AIDS since I was two. Until I was four years old, I spent a few days in the hospital every month. I had infections in my sinuses and in my pancreas. Once I had to stay in the hospital for almost a month. My grandmother didn't think I was going to live past the age of three. But I've made it to ten so far.

I've known that I have AIDS since I was six. My grandmother didn't want to lie to me. "I wanted to be truthful with you," she said. We call it "my disease." I don't like calling it by its name.

14

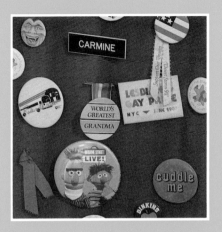

My disease is a pretty new one, not like chicken pox or the measles, which have been around for a long time. AIDS was first identified in 1983.

There is no cure for AIDS. But every year the treatments get better and better. I have tried all kinds of pills and remedies so I can get better. I've even taken medicine that is still being tested to see if it works.

I don't tell everyone what I have. Some people may not understand. When some of my grandmother's friends found out about me, they wouldn't talk to her anymore. "It's their loss, not mine," she said. Now we only tell a few people. If they don't understand, there's nothing I can do about it.

I CAN'T GO TO SCHOOL with other kids. I went to a public school for preschool, kindergarten, and first grade. I liked that, but now I have a tutor who comes to my house. Other students can't get AIDS from me, but I could catch a cold or the chicken pox from them, and then I would get very sick. My body can't fight infections. And I don't know how the other kids would react if they knew I had AIDS.

Ellen Juro is my tutor. She comes over on Mondays, Wednesdays, and Fridays. She works for the New York City Board of Education. She teaches me social studies, history, science, math, spelling, and reading. My favorite subject is science. I like reading about plants and animals, and I like solving math problems. If I live to be thirty, I have to be able to count and spell and know things like everyone else.

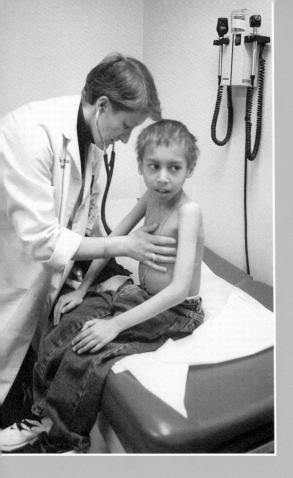

ONCE A MONTH I have to go
to Beth Israel Hospital in
New York City so the doctors
can see how I'm doing. I sit
in when the doctors have
conferences with my
grandmother. We also go to
Mount Sinai Medical Center
in Manhattan once or twice a
month. My favorite doctor is
Lea Davies, and I like to visit
with nurse Gloria Xanthos. I
have my heart checked out
and then I breathe into a
machine to see how well my
lungs are working. It's called a
spirometer.

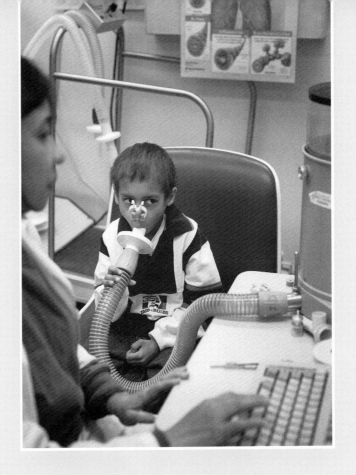

I also go to the National Cancer Institute in Maryland, where they give me different kinds of drugs to keep me going. Sometimes I take ten different pills a day. This has been my normal routine since I was born. I don't know how it is for other people.

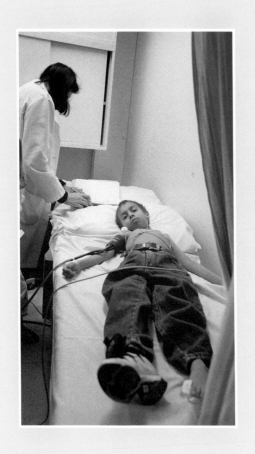

I get an infusion of blood once a month. It's called gamma globulin, and it boosts my energy. I feel better afterward. Sometimes it's hard for the nurse to find a vein to put the tube into because my veins are weak from medication and treatments. I used to have to go to the hospital to have the infusion, and it took a whole day. Now it only takes two hours.

I don't cry when I'm getting the blood. I like it when nurse Kathleen Reilly reads to me and massages my feet when I get my infusion. I like it when she tickles my toes.

MY BEST FRIENDS ARE MY COUSINS. They're the only friends I have. Danielle is ten, like me, Paul is seven, and Tara is almost three. Tara loves me so much, she keeps kissing and kissing me. We all play card games, checkers, and video games, and we draw in coloring books.

My favorite holiday is
Halloween, because my
cousins and I go trick-or-
treating. I just wish I had
more energy to play. I'm used
to spending a lot of time by
myself, so I kind of like my
peace and quiet after
they leave.

I like Pepsi, fish crackers, pizza, and Kentucky Fried Chicken. My favorite food is chicken. I try to eat as much as I can. I just gained two pounds, so now I weigh 34 pounds. Three times a week an agency called God's Love We Deliver drops off freshly cooked meals for me and other people with AIDS.

I'm a member of the Gay Men's Health Crisis. It's not just for gay men. The group organizes parties and other stuff for kids with AIDS, and they also have a lot of information about AIDS.

If I grow up big, I want to be an actor like Steven Seagal. I used to have a ponytail just like him, but I like my new haircut better. I want to get married someday. And I want to buy a car. When I have a wife, my grandmother will sit in the back seat.

My best, best friend is Dee. She's a home health aide who has special training in caring for people with AIDS. She's here for 12 hours a day, every day of the week. She's from Jamaica and she has three kids, one who's 18, another who's 21, and one who's 10—that's me! We go to the movies and play cards together. And Dee helps me with my homework. I love the chicken with curry and onions that she cooks for me.

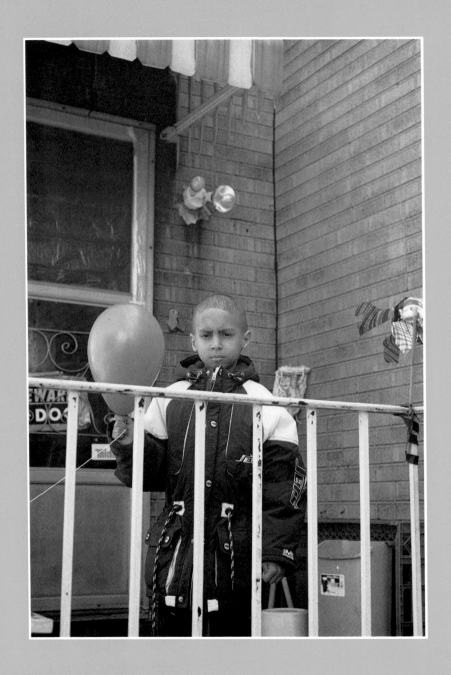

I really hope that someone finds a cure for AIDS. I think it might be too late for me. I know that I'm dying. I'm not afraid. I just don't want to be in a lot of pain. And I want to be at home in my room when the time comes.

At night, when it's quiet and the lights are out, I talk to my grandmother. Sometimes we lie in her bed and I tell her that I'll be up in heaven with my mother. Every year on my mother's birthday, I send her a balloon. I stand on my porch and let it go.

I don't like saying goodbye. I've always been like that. I
don't want people to say goodbye to me, I just want them to
send me a balloon. Lots of them.

EPILOGUE

Carmine Buete died on July 13, 1996.

He will be missed by his grandmother, Kay, his uncle, Chuck, his cousins, Danielle, Paul, and Tara, and those who knew him, especially his best friend, Dee.

They'll send up balloons to Carmine every year on May 8, his birthday.

Information about **AIDS**

Anyone can get AIDS. The disease affects people who are rich, poor, black, white, Hispanic, Asian—anyone from a basketball player to an actor to a doctor. Men and women, girls and boys have gotten AIDS. Millions of people around the world have been infected with the AIDS virus.

AIDS stands for *a*cquired *i*mmuno*d*eficiency *s*yndrome. The virus that causes AIDS is called HIV, which stands for *h*uman *i*mmuno-deficiency *v*irus. The virus attacks the body's immune system, which works to fight off infections.

People can get AIDS by having sex with someone who has the virus or by sharing needles through drug use. A mother who is HIV positive can pass the virus to her child before the child is born.

Once people have HIV, they have it for the rest of their lives. A person can be HIV positive and not have AIDS. It usually takes about ten years for a person with HIV to develop AIDS. For children, it happens more quickly, after about two years.

It's not AIDS itself that kills people. People who have the disease have a weak immune system. Their bodies can't fight off illnesses, such as pneumonia or tuberculosis or cancer. They die from these illnesses.

You can't catch AIDS like you catch a cold or the flu. You can't get it by hugging or kissing someone or by shaking hands. The virus doesn't live outside the body.

There is no vaccine to prevent people from getting AIDS. People with AIDS take different medications to help treat the infections that develop. There is no cure for AIDS. Scientists are working hard to understand how HIV works and to find a cure.

Many people who are HIV positive live healthy lives for a long time.

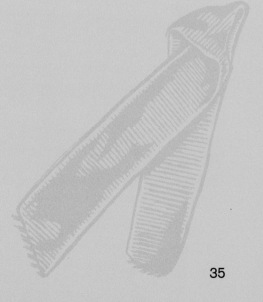

GLOSSARY

AIDS—acquired immunodeficiency syndrome; a disease caused by the human immunodeficiency virus (HIV). HIV causes a person's immune system to stop working, and the body can no longer fight off diseases.

blood transfusion (tranz-FEW-zhun)—receiving blood that was donated by another person; the blood is put in a tube called an IV, which is inserted into a vein.

cell—the smallest part of living matter that functions by itself

gamma globulin (GAM-muh GLOB-yoo-lihn)—part of the blood that provides antibodies, boosting the immune system

gay—homosexual; someone who is attracted to a person of the same sex

germs—tiny living things that can make people feel sick. Bacteria and viruses are types of germs.

heroin (HARE-oh-inn)—a strongly addictive drug; using heroin is against the law.

HIV—human immunodeficiency virus; the virus that attacks the human immune system and causes AIDS.

HIV positive—having HIV in one's bloodstream

immune system—a part of the body that protects people from diseases

infect—to give or get a disease

infusion (in-FEW-zhun)—putting a liquid, such as blood, slowly into the body, usually through a vein

pancreas (PAN-cree-uss)—a gland in the body that helps digest food

pneumonia (new-MOH-nyuh)—a disease of the lungs

sinuses (SY-nuh-suz)—air cavities in the skull behind the nostrils

spirometer (SPY-roh-mee-ter)—a machine that measures breathing

T cells—cells that are part of the immune system and act to warn the body that a virus has entered the body

vaccine (vack-SEEN)—medicine given to prevent a person from getting a particular disease

virus (VY-russ)—a type of germ that causes disease

For Further READING

Flynn, Tom, and Karen Lound. *AIDS: Examining the Crisis.*
  Minneapolis: Lerner Publications Company, 1995.
Ford, Michael Thomas. *The Voices of AIDS: Twelve Unforgettable
  People Talk about How AIDS Has Changed Their Lives.* New York:
  Morrow Junior Books, 1995.
Hyde, Margaret O., and Elizabeth H. Forsyth, M.D. *Know About
  AIDS.* Rev. ed. New York: Walker & Co., 1994.
Lerman-Golomb, Barbara. *AIDS.* Austin, Tex.: Raintree Steck-
  Vaughn, 1995.
McNaught, Denise. *The Gift of Good-Bye: A Workbook for Children
  Who Love Someone with AIDS.* New York: Delta/National
  Children's Grief Center, 1993.
Moutoussamy-Ashe, Jeanne. *Daddy and Me: A Photo Story of Arthur
  Ashe and His Daughter, Camera.* New York: Knopf, 1993.
White, Ryan, and Ann Marie Cunningham. *Ryan White: My Own
  Story.* New York: Dial Books, 1991.

For Teachers and Parents
Hausherr, Rosmarie. *Children and the AIDS Virus: A Book for
  Children, Parents and Teachers.* New York: Clarion Books, 1989.
Quackenbush, Marcia, and Sylvia Villarreal. *Does AIDS Hurt?
  Educating Young Children About AIDS.* Santa Cruz, CA: ETR
  Associates, 1992.

RESOURCES

CDC National HIV and AIDS Hotline: (800) 342-AIDS

AIDS Action
1875 Connecticut Ave. NW, Suite 700
Washington, D.C. 20009
(202) 986-1300

American Foundation for AIDS Research
733 Third Ave., 12th Floor
New York, NY 10017
(800) 392-6327

Gay Men's Health Crisis
129 W. 20th St.
New York, NY 10011
(212) 807-6655

Mothers' Voices
165 W. 46th St., Suite 701
New York, NY 10036
(212) 730-2777

National Association of People with AIDS
1413 K St. NW, 7th Floor
Washington, D.C. 20005
(202) 898-0414

National Pediatric and Family HIV Resource Center
15 S. Ninth St.
Newark, NJ 07107
(800) 362-0071

Pediatric AIDS Foundation
1311 Colorado Ave.
Santa Monica, CA 90404
(310) 395-9051

About the AUTHOR and PHOTOGRAPHER

Arlene Schulman is an award-winning journalist and photojournalist who lives in New York City. She is the author of another book for young readers, *Muhammad Ali: Champion,* and a book for adults, *The Prizefighters: An Intimate Look at Champions and Contenders.* Her work has appeared in *The New York Times, The New York Daily News, The New York Post,* and other publications. Her photographs are in the collections of The New York Public Library, the Museum of the City of New York, The Westinghouse Corporation, and private collections.